BERT THE SHIRT

written and illustrated

by

Ray Lawford

Illustrations: Ray Lawford

Publishing partner: Paragon Publishing, Rothersthorpe

ISBN 978-1-78792-084-2

Book design, layout and production management by Into Print
www.intoprint.net
+44 (0)1604 832149

This book belongs to

. . . .

BERT AND HIS FRIENDS

Bert the shirt is a very happy shirt because he lives in a clothes shop with lots of clothes and is friendly with quite a lot of them. He has some best friends as well.

The clothes in the shop that know Bert, like him because he is kind to them. He helps them if they look unhappy or feeling lonely or just want to have a talk.

Bunty the blouse and her friends are quite close by to Bert and his friends in the shop. She has also got some best friends like Bert.

She likes Bert because he is always cheerful and nice to all the clothes.

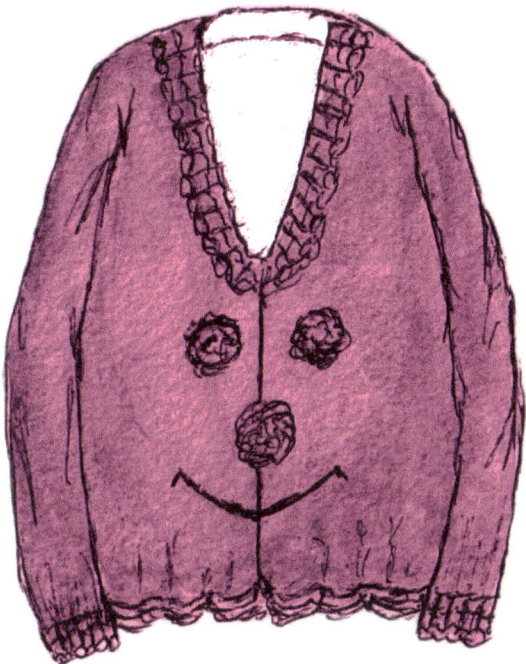

There are lots of clothes for boys in the shop. They are laid on shelves or hung on coat hangers so the people shopping can see them all.

There are shirts, trousers, socks, jumpers, T shirts and shoes. There are different colours of shirts and some have stripes and some have dots. Some are a plain colour like Bert. He is a lovely blue colour, the colour of the sky.

Close by is Bunty the blouse with the girls' clothes. Bunty is a pretty pink with lots of frills. There are blouses, skirts, dresses, sandals, jumpers and T shirts in different colours for the girls. There are blouses of yellow, green and pink just like Bunty. They are displayed on shelves and coat hangers just like the boys' clothes.

Bert's best friends are Jim the jeans, Stripy and Stripes the socks and Sam and Sammy the shoes.

They all live together on a dummy made of plastic so the people shopping can see some of the lovely boys' clothes they can buy.

They feel *very* smart.

Bunty has lots of friends and her best friends are Sue the skirt, Betty the belt and Straps and Strappy the sandals. They all live together on a dummy made of plastic so the shoppers can see some of the lovely girls' clothes that are in the shop to buy.

They feel *very* pretty standing on display.

When boys and girls see clothes they would like to have bought for them they go to a changing room to try them on to make sure they like them before their grown ups buy them.

When clothes are bought and taken home it makes their friends a little sad to see them go but the shopkeeper soon brings more clothes to put in their place and the clothes feel happy again and make new friends.

FUN TIME

At night after the shop has closed the boy clothes come alive and some jump off their coat hangers and shelves and meet in the changing rooms. They talk about things that have happened during the day and laugh about some of the things the shoppers say and do when they look at them.

Also the girls' clothes come alive and some of them go and join the boys' clothes and share their stories of the things that have happened during their day.

They sing and dance and have a lovely time.

The clothes are very happy to have such a lot of friends but they feel sorry for the clothes who do not have friends and who look rather sad. They hope they will be able to make them happy as well.

Bunty said to Bert

"We should talk to the clothes who don't have any friends and tell them about our fun together and how happy we are."

"That is a good idea" Bert said. *"We should try and get them to come to our fun times and join in."*

Long before the cleaning people come into the shop early the next morning the clothes all hurry back to their shelves and coat hangers as if nothing had happened.

SATURDAYS

Saturdays are always the busiest day of the week in the shop and Bert wondered why.

Bunty said

"It's because lots of grown ups have to go somewhere called work on the other days of the week so Saturdays is when they like to go shopping with their children."

It is also a very busy time for all the clothes because they are being looked at, picked up, pulled about and sometimes tried on to see what they look like. Most shoppers are quite careful and put them back if they don't want to buy them.

Some shoppers are not quite so careful and leave some of the clothes untidy or put them back in the wrong place.

This makes the clothes quite unhappy.

Bert and his best friends care about all their friends and are happy when they see kind shoppers tidy their friends and put them back in the right place.

This makes the clothes happy again.

SALES

Sometimes the shopkeeper has something called a sale. This means the shopkeeper wants to get shoppers to buy more clothes and so he makes some of them cheaper. The clothes in the sale are not very happy because they are cheaper. It makes them feel not as important as the clothes that are not in the sale. Also the clothes in the sale are all put together so they are away from their friends.

As soon as the shop doors are opened lots of shoppers rush in and push one another about so they can get to the clothes first. They pull the clothes about and take them off their coat hangers to have a better look and try them on. Some of the clothes get left on the floor and feel that no one cares about them.

If Bert sees clothes getting upset or left on the floor he feels sorry for them. He waits until no one is looking and says to Jim the jeans, Stripy and Stripes the socks and Sam and Sammy the shoes

  "Let us jump down off our plastic dummy and help the clothes and put them back."

This makes the clothes much happier and grateful to Bert the shirt and his best friends for helping them.

After the sale is over all the clothes in the sale are put back with all of their friends and they are all happy again.

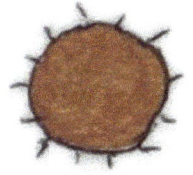

WINDOW DISPLAY

Some of the clothes started getting quite excited because they had heard whispers that something special is going to happen in the shop.

"We wonder what it could be and what is going to happen?" they say.

Soon the shopkeeper went into the shop with his helpers and into the big shop window and started looking around, talking and pointing and getting quite excited.

Bert and his best friends, Jim, Sam, Sammy and Stripe and Stripy were trying to guess what was going to happen but it was a mystery. They would have to wait and find out.

The next day the shopkeeper and his two helpers went into the big window again carrying boxes full of pretty things like trees, flowers, grass, a sun and fluffy white clouds.

They were working for quite a long time. When they had finished they stood back to look at their work and were very pleased with what they had done.

Bert and his best friends were just close enough to have a peek at what had been done in the window. It was very clever. They had made the window display look like a pretty garden.

Bert said to Jim

"It looks like a summer day."

What is that all for? they wondered.

They would have to wait a little longer to find out.

BERT AND BUNTY'S SURPRISE

The helpers came back into the shop and went to the plastic dummies and carried Bert and Bunty and their best friends into the big window display and put them in the summer scene. It was getting very exciting.

Bunty, Sue, Betty, Straps and Strappy all felt extra pretty and Bert, Jim, Stripy, Stripes, Sam and Sammy felt extra smart.

It wasn't very long before lots of people walking by stopped to look at them and say how lovely they all looked. Many passersby went into the shop to see what they would buy. All the clothes felt very important. They would have to be on their best behaviour.

NIGHT TIME

Each night when the shop has closed and it is dark the shopkeeper goes into the window and switches on the lights so the people passing by outside can still see the lovely clothes in the shop window.

This means the clothes cannot all get together with each other like they can in the shop when no one is about because people passing by would see. They could talk together guietly when no one was watching and talk about all the people they had seen looking in the window and the things they were saying about the display and the clothes.

BACK TO THE SHOP

After about three weeks the shop keeper came into the window with his helpers and said it was time to change the window display. They took the trees, flowers, grass, the sun and the fluffy white clouds out of the window.

This meant that Bert and Bunty and their best friends were also taken back into the shop which made them sad because they had all been so happy together in the window.

Then they heard the shopkeeper say that because Bert and his best friends and Bunty and her best friends looked so good together in the shop window they could still stay next to each other in the shop.

Bert the shirt, Bunty the blouse and their best friends were all so happy they could still be together.

GREY JUMPERS

A **few** days later the shopkeeper came into the shop with some grey jumpers. He put some on the shelf and he hung three up on hangers near to Bunty, Sue, Betty, Straps and Strappy. The jumpers looked as if they might not be very friendly. Bunty smiled at the three on the hangers to see if they would smile back but they just pulled faces and stared at a lot of the clothes.

Bert and his friends could see the girls' clothes didn't look happy.

That night Bert and his best friends went with Bunty and her best friends to meet some of the other clothes who had gone to the changing room to all get together like they often did. They had also managed to persuade some of the clothes who didn't have friends to join them. But then the three grey jumpers also came and joined them.

The jumpers started laughing at the nice clothes and calling them nasty names, said they looked silly in their fancy clothes and bright colours.

Bert saw what was happening and said to the girls' clothes

   "Don't listen to the jumpers and don't say anything to them."

Soon the grey jumpers saw the clothes were not listening to them so they stopped being nasty and went back to their place in the shop.

AUTUMN

It was not long before the shop keeper and his helpers went back into the window display with more boxes. They took in lots of brown leaves, twigs and tree branches and made a window display with them. The shop keeper said it was to make the display look like autumn. Bert wondered what autumn was.

Jim said

"I think it is autumn when the leaves go brown and fall off the trees."

AUTUMN JACKETS

The shop keeper and his helpers took jackets into the window. Then they took Bert, his best friends and Bunty and her best friends on their plastic dummies into the window and put them in the autumn display. Bert and Bunty and their friends wondered what was going to happen next and what is was all about. Then the helpers put a lovely brown jacket on Bert. They put a pretty pink jacket on Bunty. Then they moved them both under a sign that said **'Autumn Jackets'**.

They all started to feel quite warm in their extra clothes and said

"Boys and girls will feel warm and cosy in these when autumn comes."

NEW FRIENDS

The jackets felt rather shy of Bert and Bunty and their best friends at first. When the shoppers had gone home that night Bert and Bunty and their best friends started to talk to the jackets to try and make them feel at home and they asked them what their names were.

After a little while the jackets started to feel less shy and started to talk to them. The jacket on Bert said *"My name is Jock"*

and the jacket on Bunty said *"My name is Jane"*.

Bert and Bunty asked the jackets where they came from because they had not seen jackets like them before. They said

> "We were made in Scotland on a special machine which makes us very warm for people to wear."

The new clothes now felt much better and were really happy to be with their new friends. They all hoped they would be able to stay together in the window for quite a lot longer so they could still enjoy seeing all the people walking by and looking in at them in the window.

AUTUMN
JACKETS

After a while it was starting to get chilly outside and so people were not stopping so long to look in the window. The shopkeeper decided to take Bert and Bunty and their best friends back into the shop where more people would look at them. The shopkeeper said they could still stay next to each other in the shop. This made them all very happy.

They all hoped there would be more adventures for them all to enjoy and wondered what they might be.

They would have to wait and see…

www.ingramcontent.com/pod-product-compliance
Lightning Source LLC
Chambersburg PA
CBHW041434040426
42452CB00020B/2972